Dragonflies

Heather C. Hudak

Published by Weigl Publishers Inc.
350 5th Avenue, Suite 3304, PMB 6G
New York, NY 10118-0069
Website: www.weigl.com

Library of Congress Cataloging-in-Publication Data

Hudak, Heather C., 1975-
 Dragonflies / Heather C. Hudak.
    p. cm. -- (World of wonder)
 Includes index.
 ISBN 978-1-59036-864-0 (hard cover : alk. paper) -- ISBN 978-1-59036-865-7 (soft cover : alk. paper)
 1. Dragonflies--Juvenile literature. I. Title.
 QL520.H83 2009
 595.7'33--dc22
                              2008023850

Printed in the United States of America
1 2 3 4 5 6 7 8 9 0 12 11 10 09 08

Editor: Heather C. Hudak
Design and Layout: Terry Paulhus

Weigl acknowledges Getty Images as its primary image supplier.

CONTENTS

What is a Dragonfly?

Have you ever seen a creature with a long body and shiny wings zip through the air? This may have been a dragonfly.

A dragonfly is a type of insect. There are more than 5,000 types of dragonfly.

Many dragonflies have wings that look like lace and glass.

6

Back in Time

The first dragonflies lived at the same time as dinosaurs! This was about 300 million years ago.

Ancient dragonflies were so large that they would barely fit through a doorway. Their wingspan was more than 2 feet (0.6 meters) wide. Today, the largest dragonflies have a wingspan of 6 inches (15 centimeters).

Dragonfly Life Cycle

A dragonfly begins life as a nymph. Nymphs hatch from eggs and live in water. They **molt** many times as they grow.

Full-grown nymphs crawl out of the water and up the stem of a plant. Their skin cracks open. The dragonfly crawls out. Blood pumps up the wings and body of a new dragonfly.

Nymph in water

Nymph on stem

Nymph skin opening

Adult out of shell

What Does a Dragonfly Look Like?

What does your body look like? It is quite different from a dragonfly. Like all insects, dragonflies have three main body parts. They have a head, a thorax, and an abdomen.

Dragonflies have a large head. Eyes, **antennae**, and jaws are found on the head. The wings and legs are attached to the thorax. The abdomen has 10 parts. It is long and slim.

head

thorax

abdomen

Incredible Eyes

Imagine if you had eyes the size of a large melon! This is what a dragonfly's eyes are like. Dragonflies have the largest eyes of any insect. They have two huge eyes that cover most of their head. These are called compound eyes. Each compound eye has up to 30,000 **lenses**. Human eyes only have one lens.

Dragonflies can see even the smallest movements.

Above and Beyond

Have you ever seen a helicopter **hover** in one place? Unlike other insects, dragonflies can hold still in one place. They can fly forward, backward, upward, downward, and turn.

Dragonflies are the fastest insects on Earth. They fly at speeds of 30 to 60 miles (48 to 97 kilometers) per hour. The fastest dragonfly recorded was soaring at 36 miles (58 km) per hour.

What's for Dinner?

Could you eat half of your body weight in one meal? Dragonflies often eat meals this size or larger.

Dragonflies are fierce hunters! They eat just about any insects they can catch. They may eat flies, mosquitoes, and midges.

Dragonflies use their legs to catch **prey** in mid-air. To do this, the dragonfly forms its legs into a basket shape. This basket acts as a net to trap flies. Dragonflies use their jaws to catch some small insects.

Wetland Homes

Dragonflies live all over the world! They can live any place that has water nearby. Ponds, rivers, lakes, streams, and swamps are perfect places for dragonflies to live. In fact, most of a dragonfly's life is spent in the water. Nymphs live in the water for about a year. Dragonflies live only a few weeks on land.

Many **predators** live in or near these water **habitats**. Birds, spiders, fish, and newts hunt dragonflies for food.

Insect Lore

Dragonflies are sometimes called the devil's **darning needles**. This is because people once thought dragonflies could sew shut the lips of a naughty child.

In some parts of the United States, people call dragonflies snake doctors. At one time, people thought these insects cared for sick snakes.

Make a Dragonfly

Supplies
construction paper in many colors, pencil, crayons or markers, scissors, glue

1. Close your fingers tight. Then, trace the palm of your hand on a sheet of paper. Cut out the handprint.

2. Repeat 11 times using different colored paper each time. You should have 12 handprints.

3. Glue the bottom of one handprint to the top of another.

4. Glue the bottom of another handprint to the top of the other two. This forms a chain. It is one of the dragonfly's wings.

5. Repeat three times so that you have four wings.

6. Draw a long triangle on a sheet of paper. Cut out the triangle.

7. Draw a circle about the same size as one of the handprints on a sheet of paper. Cut out the circle.

8. Glue the flat part of the triangle to the bottom of the circle.

9. Glue one of the wings on the back the circle where it meets the triangle. Repeat on the other side.

10. Glue one of the wings on the back of triangle just below the other wing. Repeat on the other side.

11. Next, draw a face on your dragonfly using crayons or markers.

12. Now you have a colorful dragonfly to hang on your wall.

Find Out More

To learn more about dragonflies, visit these websites.

Desert USA
www.desertusa.com/mag98/
nov/papr/drangonflies.html

**Environmental
Education for Kids**
www.dnr.state.wi.us/org/
caer/ce/eek/critter/
insect/dragonfly.htm

Nature North
www.naturenorth.com/
dragonfly/DOM/Page
01_Biology.html

FEATURE SITE:
www.biokids.umich.edu/
critters/Anisoptera

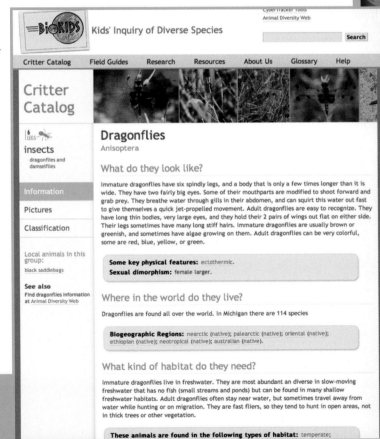

BioKIDS Kids' Inquiry of Diverse Species

Cyber Tracker Tools
Animal Diversity Web

Search

Critter Catalog   Field Guides   Research   Resources   About Us   Glossary   Help

Critter Catalog

6 LEGS

insects
dragonflies and
damselflies

Information

Pictures

Classification

Local animals in this group:
black saddlebags

See also
Find dragonflies information at Animal Diversity Web

Dragonflies
Anisoptera

What do they look like?

Immature dragonflies have six spindly legs, and a body that is only a few times longer than it is wide. They have two fairly big eyes. Some of their mouthparts are modified to shoot forward and grab prey. They breathe water through gills in their abdomen, and can squirt this water out fast to give themselves a quick jet-propelled movement. Adult dragonflies are easy to recognize. They have long thin bodies, very large eyes, and they hold their 2 pairs of wings out flat on either side. Their legs sometimes have many long stiff hairs. Immature dragonflies are usually brown or greenish, and sometimes have algae growing on them. Adult dragonflies can be very colorful, some are red, blue, yellow, or green.

Some key physical features: ectothermic.
Sexual dimorphism: female larger.

Where in the world do they live?

Dragonflies are found all over the world. In Michigan there are 114 species

Biogeographic Regions: nearctic (native); palearctic (native); oriental (native); ethiopian (native); neotropical (native); australian (native).

What kind of habitat do they need?

Immature dragonflies live in freshwater. They are most abundant an diverse in slow-moving freshwater that has no fish (small streams and ponds) but can be found in many shallow freshwater habitats. Adult dragonflies often stay near water, but sometimes travel away from water while hunting or on migration. They are fast fliers, so they tend to hunt in open areas, not in thick trees or other vegetation.

These animals are found in the following types of habitat: temperate;

Glossary

antennae: long, slim feelers found on the head

darning needles: long sewing needles that have a large eye and are used to mend clothing

habitats: the places where an animal lives in nature

hover: hang in one place

lenses: clear substances that are curved to bend light

molt: to shed skin or fur

predators: animals that hunt other animals for food

prey: animals that are hunted by other animals

Index